CERITA WILANGAN

THE NUMBER STORY

SMALL BOOK ONE

ENGLISH - JAVANESE

Numbers Teach Children
Their Number Names

written and illustrated by

MISS ANNA

Early Reader Edition of *The Number Story 1*
Bronze Medal Winner, 2016 Wishing Shelf Book Award

Library of Congress Control Number: 2018902040

Names: Miss Anna, author.
Title: Number story : numbers teach children their number names / Miss Anna.
Description: Portland, OR: Lumpy Publishing, 2018.
Identifiers: ISBN 978-1-945977-64-0 | LCCN 2018902040
Summary: The pictures and rhymes present stories which introduce numbers 0-10.
Subjects: LCSH Numeration—English--Javanese--Pictorial works--Juvenile literature. | BISAC JUVENILE NONFICTION /
Languages: English--Javanese
Classification: LCC QA141.3 .M57 2018 | DDC 513—dc23

Publisher: Lumpy Publishing
Website: www.missannabooks.com
Email: missanna@missannabooks.com

Paperback: ISBN 978-1-945977-64-0
Printed in the U.S.A.   1 3 5 7 9 10 8 6 4 2

Kersa sinau nami
wilangan kita?

It is very easy and a lot of fun!

Gampil sanget uga
ngrenakaken sanget!

Say-along our little jingle

Ucapke sareng jingle alit kita!

Nyanyi sareng kita!

starting from Number One!

Kita badhe awiti saking

wilangan setunggal!

1

ONE looks like my one finger.

SETUNGGAL

Punika leres kados driji kula.

1
ONE!
SETUNGGAL!

2

TWO   trails a tail.

KALIH

nggadhahi bunthut.

SETUNGGAL BUNTHUT!

3

THREE   has bumps.

TIGO
Punika mlengkung.

Punika kados setunggal bukit!

BERGELOMBANG!   MLENGKUNG!

4

FOUR carries a sail.

SEKAWAN

Punika kapal layar.

A SAIL!
Setunggal kapal
kaliyan Layar!

5

FIVE   is a racing track.

GANGSAL
Punika lintasan balap.

VROOM
VROOM
VROOOM !

6

ENEM

Punika mlengkung kados siput.

SETUNGGAL
SIPUT!

A SNAIL!

7

SEVEN has a sharp angle.

PITU

Punika kapak.

BE CAREFUL! IT IS SHARP!

NGATOS-ATOS! PUNIKA TAJEM!

8

EIGHT is rollercoaster rails.

WOLU
Punika *rollercoaster*.

HURA!
YIPPEE!

NINE   is a bubble on a stick.

SANGA

Punika gelembung ing teken.

A BUBBLE!
SETUNGGAL GELEMBUNG!

TEN   is an eye of a whale.

SADASA

Punika mripat paus.

NGEDHEPAKEN!
WINK!
HELLO! HALO!

And
Uga
0
ZERO   is an empty pail.
NOL
Punika ember kosong.

IT'S
EMPTY!
NIKI
KOSONG!

Thank you for playing with us today.

We had a lot of fun too!

Matur nuwun sampun dolanan
kaliyan kita dinten niki.
Kita ugi rena-rena!

We are your Number friends,
Zero to Ten,
Who will be here for you~
Kita rencang panjenengan
Nol ngantos Sadasa.
Kita badhe enten ing
mriki konjuk panjenengan~

Bye-bye now!
See you again soon!
Wilujeng tilar sakmenika!
Ngantos kepanggih malih!

The Numbers are *SINGING* too!

To sing-a-long, look for Miss Anna Number Story
at your favorite music store like iTUNES.

MP3

Numbers 0-10
IDENTIFYING
& COUNTING

Numbers 11-20
& Ordinals
first, second, third...

Numbers 0-100
& Place Values
ones, tens, hundreds...

About Clocks
& Telling Time
hours, minutes, seconds

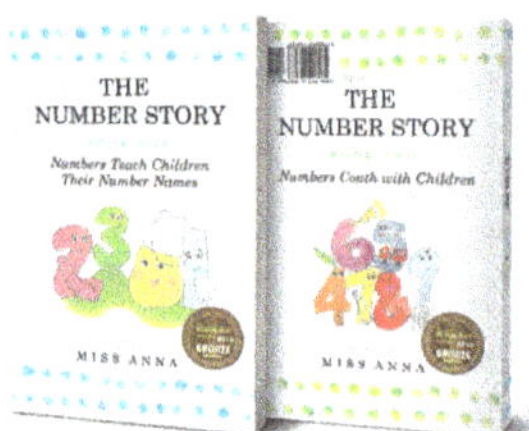

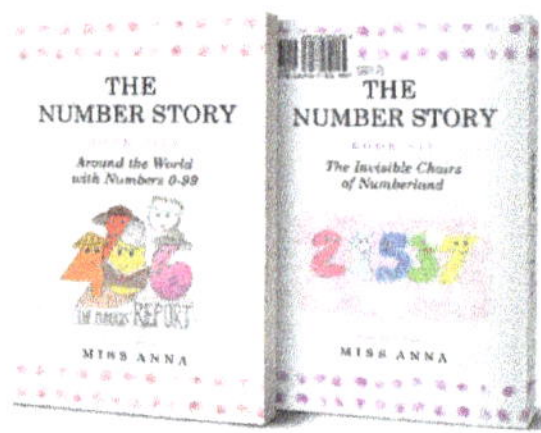

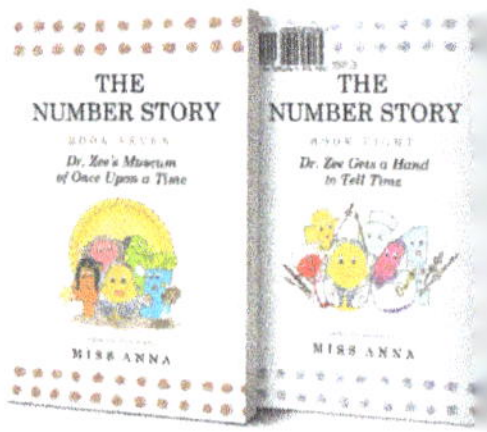

Number Story 1 & 2
isbn: 978-0-996216-48-7

Number Story 3 & 4
isbn: 978-1-945977-01-5

Number Story 5 & 6
isbn: 978-1-945977-06-0

Number Story 7 & 8
isbn: 978-1-949320-40-

For more Miss Anna books to love,
visit us at

www.missannabooks.com

Numbers are working hard all over the world!
Come Travel the World with Us!